Exclusively

PRESIDENTIAL

TRIVIA

by Anthony S. Pitch

Mino Publications
Potomac, Md.

Published by

Mino Publications
9009 Paddock Lane
Potomac, MD 20854

Library of Congress Catalog Card
No. 84-62716

ISBN 0-931719-01-1

Printed in the United States of America

To the memory of my parents,
Chummy and Ivor,
Who enriched the lives of so many,
And for whom no tribute of mine
Can express the measure of my admiration

1. Why did English Puritans toss out of his parish the clergyman great-great grandfather of George Washington?

2. From which British monarch was Richard Nixon descended?

3. What were Bill Clinton's birth names?

4. Why was Herbert Hoover's likeness not included in the series of postage stamps of all former Presidents, brought out in 1938, long after he was Chief Executive?

5. What request did Gerald Ford make of his helicopter pilot on his last day as President?

6. Which President remained a lifelong bachelor?

7. How did Theodore Roosevelt turn the tables on an anti-Semitic demagogue demanding police protection for a speech in New York?

8. Guess which President placed a sign on his Oval Office desk reading *It CAN be done*?

ANSWERS

1. They said he was drunk too often

2. King Edward III (1312–1377)

3. William Jefferson Blythe

4. A Federal law forbade the likeness of a living person from being reproduced on any U.S. security

5. To circle slowly over the dome of the Capitol

6. James Buchanan

7. Roosevelt, then New York Police Commissioner, assigned only Jewish policemen to protect the demagogue

8. Ronald Reagan

9. How did Harry Truman learn he was President?

10. Which President lived in retirement at the swank Waldorf Towers in New York City?

11. Lyndon Johnson made history when he appointed this man to the Supreme Court. Why?

12. What was eerie about Presidential elections held every 20 years from 1840 to 1960?

13. What was the temperature of the White House indoor pool in which John Kennedy swam almost daily?

14. Why was Captain Ulysses S. Grant asked to resign from the army?

15. What heroic act took the life of a Presidential candidate?

16. On what occasion did the Marine Band make its first public appearance at an official ceremony?

17. On what floor of the White House are the living quarters of the First Family?

ANSWERS

9. Eleanor Roosevelt told him her husband had just died

10. Herbert Hoover

11. Thurgood Marshall was the first black to sit on the Supreme Court

12. The person elected in 1840, 1860, 1880, 1900, 1920, 1940 and 1960 died in office

13. 90 degrees fahrenheit

14. Because he was drunk so often

15. In 1928 the Socialist Labor nominee, Frank Johns, drowned in a river while trying to rescue a boy

16. The second inaugural of President James Monroe

17. The second floor

18. How many animals did former President Theodore Roosevelt shoot during his 11-month trek in Africa?

19. Who was the *first* President born in a log cabin?

20. First Lady Grace Coolidge had a most unusual pet called Rebecca. What was it?

21. Which victim of an assassin implored by-standers to spare the murderer exclaiming: "Let no one hurt him"?

22. Which incumbent President, aged 54, married the 20-year-old daughter of his Secretary of the Navy?

23. Which financially-strapped former President was turned down for a loan by the Bank of the United States?

24. What was the name of the coquette who so turned the head of Thomas Jefferson that he jumped over a fence, caught his foot and permanently damaged his right hand?

25. How soon after becoming President did Harry Truman get briefed on the secret development of the atomic bomb?

ANSWERS

18. 296

19. Andrew Jackson

20. A tame raccoon

21. President William McKinley

22. President John Tyler

23. James Madison

24. Mrs. Maria Cosway

25. Half an hour

26. Why did Spiro Agnew go to a Maryland funeral home the day he resigned as Vice President?

27. How long was Ronald Reagan married to his first wife, Jane Wyman?

28. Name the Oxford University college attended by Bill Clinton.

29. Which President wrote in his diary that he was the hardest working man in the country?

30. How much money did Dwight Eisenhower net from his book *Crusade in Europe?*

31. Was it coincidence that two of President Cleveland's brothers died on the same day in the same year?

32. What was President Chester Arthur's favorite recreation?

33. Which President doted on his epileptic wife?

34. How many books did George Washington own at the time of his death?

ANSWERS

26. The body of his half-brother, who had died a few days earlier, was awaiting burial

27. Eight years

28. University College

29. James Polk

30. $476,000

31. No. They were both aboard a ship bound for Cuba when it caught fire

32. Salmon fishing

33. William McKinley

34. 884 according to his executors' inventory

35. What unique tragedy befell Theodore Roosevelt on St. Valentine's Day?

36. How old was Bill Clinton when he became the youngest Governor in the U.S.?

37. Iowan-born Herbert Hoover stands forever in U.S. history books because of his place of birth. Why?

38. How old was Franklin Roosevelt when he was crippled by polio?

39. What was the name of the renegade Republican Senator from Kansas whose not-guilty votes saved President Andrew Johnson from being convicted in his impeachment trial?

40. How long did surgeons try to resuscitate President Kennedy before he was declared dead?

41. What was the name of President Ford's golden retriever pet dog?

42. What made General Eisenhower mad when he met General Montgomery in the Briton's headquarters?

ANSWERS

35. In separate rooms in the same Manhattan house, his mother died of typhoid and, 11 hours later, his first wife died after giving birth to a daughter the day before

36. 32

37. He was the first President born west of the Mississippi

38. 39

39. Edmund G. Ross

40. About 30 minutes

41. Liberty

42. Non-smoker Montgomery forbade the chain-smoking Eisenhower from lighting up in the headquarters

43. At what inopportune moment did a cap fall off one of President Nixon's teeth?

44. Did Jimmy Carter act spontaneously in stopping his limousine to walk the remainder of his inaugural route to the White House?

45. How did Eleanor Roosevelt learn of the deep attachment between her husband and Lucy Mercer?

46. What was written on a banner strung across the *Washington Post* building immediately after Harry Truman won the 1948 election?

47. Who hollered inside India's Taj Mahal to listen to his echo?

48. How many state capitals are named after Presidents?

49. How heavy was William Howard Taft at his inauguration?

50. Which assassin's cervical vertebrae and spinal cord are displayed in the Armed Forces Institute of Pathology at Walter Reed Hospital, Washington, D.C.?

ANSWERS

43. The night he won reelection to a second term and had to make a TV appearance

44. No. He had decided in advance to walk to dramatize the new open presidency

45. She found letters from Mercer to FDR

46. *Mr. President, we are ready to eat crow whenever you are ready to serve it*

47. Vice President Lyndon Johnson

48. Four: Jackson, Miss.; Jefferson City, Mo.; Lincoln, Neb.; Madison, Wis.

49. 332 lbs.

50. John Wilkes Booth, who shot Abraham Lincoln

51. What was the effect of the 22nd Amendment, ratified in 1951?

52. The Secret Service gave these code names to a) George H.W. Bush   b) Bill Clinton

53. Why was Jacqueline Kennedy absent from the Democratic Party's Convention which nominated her husband in 1960?

54. Young George W. Bush was given this nickname at Phillips Academy in Andover, Massachusetts, because he was not shy about voicing his opinions

55. Why did Jimmy Carter work in the White House kitchen under Franklin Roosevelt?

56. Which portraits of former Presidents did Lyndon Johnson hang in the Oval Office?

57. Which former President rejected, a few months before his death, an offer to be buried in the marble sarcophagus that had once held the remains of a Roman emperor?

58. With whom did Ronald and Nancy Reagan spend their honeymoon?

ANSWERS

51. It limited Presidential tenure to two terms

52. a) Timberwolf b) Eagle

53. She was pregnant

54. "Lip"

55. This was the name of the live-in White House chef

56. George Washington, Andrew Jackson, Franklin Roosevelt

57. Andrew Jackson, who said his Republican feelings and principles forbade it

58. Her parents

59. What was Gerald Ford's regular breakfast menu at the White House?

60. During whose administration did U.S.
combat deaths in Vietnam surpass the
33,629 killed in the Korean War?

61. What arrangements had Harry Truman
made for evening entertainment before he
learned he had succeeded to the
Presidency?

62. Which poem by Alan Seeger was one of
John Kennedy's favorites?

63. What real estate deal linked President
Martin Van Buren and British Prime
Minister Winston Churchill?

64. Who were nicknamed *The American Kings?*

65. Who died of wounds sustained in a duel
two days after hosting a wedding ball for
the daughter of President Monroe?

66. Name the only President born on the
Fourth of July.

67. List, in order, the 5 persons in line of
succession to the Presidency.

59. Grapefruit, English muffin and tea

60. In the first months of Richard Nixon's Presidency

61. He had arranged a game of poker

62. *I Have a Rendezvous with Death*

63. Van Buren's home, 18 miles south of Albany, N.Y., was later bought by Leonard Jerome, maternal grandfather of Churchill

64. The first five Presidents, whose faces were well known through engraved reproductions of portraits by Gilbert Stuart

65. Commodore Stephen Decatur

66. Calvin Coolidge

67. i) Vice President
    ii) Speaker of the House of Representatives
   iii) President Pro Tempore of the Senate
    iv) Secretary of State
     v) Secretary of the Treasury

68. What did Thomas Jefferson's grandchildren call him?

69. What was Woodrow Wilson's thesis for his Ph.D.?

70. What title did 18th century Senators propose for the President before Congressmen objected?

71. Why did fellow officers nickname the youthful Ulysses S. Grant *The Little Beauty?*

72. Who gave the briefest inaugural address?

73. How many Presidents died without leaving a will?

74. Why did Mary Todd Lincoln race down Pennsylvania Avenue in a carriage on the morning of her husband's inauguration?

75. What momentous event fell on Harry Truman's 61st birthday?

76. Did Richard Nixon, with a total of four, have the most Attorneys General?

77. What promise did First Lady Ellen Wilson seek from her physician on her death bed?

68. Grandpapa

69. *Congressional Government*

70. *His Highness the President of the U.S.A. & Protector of their Liberties.*

71. Because his complexion was then girlish

72. George Washington spoke only 135 words at his second inaugural

73. Four: Lincoln, Andrew Johnson, Grant, and Garfield

74. Lincoln had gone to the Capitol early to work and she suddenly realized he would not be returning to the White House before the inauguration

75. His announcement of the unconditional surrender of Germany and the end of World War II in Europe

76. No. Ulysses S. Grant had five Attorneys General. Other Presidents who had four were Thomas Jefferson, Franklin Roosevelt and Harry Truman

77. To take good care of her husband, Woodrow Wilson

78. Where is the home in which Warren Harding lived until he entered the White House in 1921?

79. Name the two Presidents who were born on the same street in the same city.

80. Which man was both 22nd and 24th President?

81. Why was James Buchanan in the habit of closing one of his eyes so often?

82. A heavy drinker all his life, this President went on the wagon four years before his death—yet still died of cirrhosis of the liver. Who was he?

83. In which movie did Nancy Reagan play opposite her husband, Ronald?

84. Who introduced Richard Nixon to Henry Kissinger at their first meeting?

85. In which building in Richmond, Va. will you find the sculptured likenesses of the eight Virginians who served as Presidents of the U.S.?

ANSWERS

78. Marion, Ohio

79. John Adams and his son, John Quincy Adams, were born on Franklin Street in Quincy, Massachusetts

80. Grover Cleveland, who was elected to non-consecutive terms

81. He was nearsighted in one eye and far-sighted in the other

82. Franklin Pierce

83. *Hellcats of the Navy*

84. Clare Boothe Luce, at her home in 1967

85. The State Capitol

86. Which President signed a check payable to a "one-legged colored man"?

87. What were the Secret Service code names for the following on the day John Kennedy was shot?
    a) John Kennedy
    b) Jacqueline Kennedy
    c) Lyndon Johnson
    d) Lady Bird Johnson
    e) The White House
    f) Air Force One

88. Who was the first President to leave the continental United States?

89. The first child born in the White House was the grandson of Thomas Jefferson. Which future President was he named after?

90. What was on the program when Jimmy Carter and Leonid Brezhnev went to the opera together in Vienna?

91. For what reason was President Eisenhower's pet dog, Heidi, banished from the White House to the General's Gettysburg farm?

ANSWERS

86. Abraham Lincoln

87. a) Lancer
    b) Lace
    c) Volunteer
    d) Victoria
    e) Castle
    f) Angel

88. Theodore Roosevelt, when he sailed to Panama in 1906

89. James Madison Randolph, born 1806, was named in honor of Jefferson's successor

90. Mozart's *Abduction from the Seraglio*

91. For urinating in the Diplomatic Reception Room

92. Why was a hand mirror held up in the hospital operating room as doctors strained to save the life of President William McKinley?

93. What do genealogists believe was the ancestral family name of President Polk?

94. How many wedding presents did Franklin and Eleanor Roosevelt get?

95. How many oval rooms are there in the White House—excluding the President's office in the West Wing?

96. What did President George Washington buy on the same day he laid the cornerstone of the Capitol?

97. Which advertising firm did Bob Haldeman take leave of absence from to join Richard Nixon's 1960 Presidential campaign?

98. How tall was the first grizzly bear shot by Theodore Roosevelt?

99. What was so unusual about the white wine drunk by Jacqueline Kennedy in the White House?

ANSWERS

92. To reflect sunlight onto the President's body because the light bulbs were so dim

93. Pollok

94. 340

95. Three: the Diplomatic Reception Room, the Blue Room, the Oval Study

96. Four lots of property in the city which eventually bore his name

97. J. Walter Thompson

98. Almost 9 ft.

99. She put ice in her glass

100. What is the length of the inaugural route between the White House and the Capitol?

101. Franklin Roosevelt's pet Scottie was named
    a) Scottie
    b) Blackie
    c) Fala

102. Which President was so sparse with words that he was known as *Silent Cal?*

103. How long did John Kennedy like his two eggs boiled for breakfast?

104. How long after his birth did Lyndon Johnson's parents finally agree on his name?

105. In which sumptuous setting did Herbert Hoover regularly dine while President?

106. When told of rumors that he had a mistress, which President gasped: "This is worse than assassination!"?

107. Why was Andrew Johnson tipsy at his inauguration as Vice President?

ANSWERS

100. 1.2 miles

101. c) Fala

102. Calvin Coolidge

103. Four minutes

104. Three months—before that he was called *the baby*

105. The State Dining Room

106. Chester Arthur

107. He had been sick for months and he drank that morning on the advice of his doctor

108. Where was Spiro Agnew when Richard Nixon asked him to be his running mate?

109. What was the title of the book Woodrow Wilson wrote on a previous President?

110. By what name is the Presidential cottage at Camp David known?

111. Where can you view the only surviving complete set of portraits of the first five Presidents, painted by Gilbert Stuart?

112. What Amendment to the Constitution provides that no one may be elected President more than twice?

113. How long did it take Thomas Jefferson's ship to cross the Atlantic from Boston to Cowes, England, on his way to France as U.S. diplomatic head?

114. How old was Nancy Reagan when Ronald Reagan first met her?

115. Whom did Harry Truman rate the five greatest Presidents of the U.S., and in what order did he place them?

ANSWERS

108. In his 12th floor suite at the Eden Roc Hotel, Miami Beach

109. *Life of George Washington*

110. Aspen

111. In the National Gallery of Art, Washington, D.C.

112. 22nd Amendment

113. 21 days

114. 28

115. a) Washington
     b) Jefferson
     c) Woodrow Wilson
     d) Lincoln
     e) Franklin Roosevelt

116. What did President Ford do immediately after pardoning Richard Nixon?

117. At what hour did Lyndon Johnson go to bed the first night of his Presidency?

118. Who wrote the introduction to John Kennedy's first book, *Why England Slept*?

119. What did the middle initial *S* stand for in Ulysses S. Grant?

120. What was the name of the horse ridden most often by George Washington during the Revolutionary War?

121. On what occasion did Franklin Roosevelt proclaim that ''the only thing we have to fear is fear itself''?

122. What political accomplishment achieved by James K. Polk remains unequalled in American history?

123. What was the value of the government bonds which Mary Todd Lincoln was forced to surrender from her underwear immediately after being judged insane?

ANSWERS

116. He drove to Burning Tree Country Club to play golf

117. 3 a.m.

118. *Time* Magazine publisher, Henry Luce

119. Simpson

120. Nelson

121. His first inaugural address

122. He was the only Speaker of the House of Representatives to have been elected President

123. $56,000

124. What did Jimmy Carter do to his hair while President?

125. How did Governor Bill Clinton regularly celebrate Thanksgiving before entering the White House?

126. By how many votes did Ronald Reagan defeat incumbent Governor Edmund Brown in the California election of 1966?

127. Who was the first TV correspondent to become White House press secretary?

128. What would many superstitious people have considered an ill omen about the first full day Harry Truman was President?

129. Of what wood was George Washington's coffin made?

130. Which signatories to the Declaration of Independence later became Presidents of the U.S.?

131. What was the name of Harry Truman's partner in their haberdashery shop in Kansas City, Missouri?

ANSWERS

124. He began parting it on the left, instead of the right

125. He served dinner to his servants then washed up

126. 993,739

127. Ron Nessen, press secretary to Gerald Ford

128. It was Friday the 13th

129. Mahogany

130. John Adams and Thomas Jefferson

131. Eddie Jacobson

132. Which President confessed himself to be a "night person"?

133. What made Rutherford Hayes note-worthy among the five Presidents who fought in the Civil War?

134. Which President took the oath of office from a woman?

135. He was the youngest U.S. naval aviator when he got his wings in 1942.

136. How did Woodrow Wilson react to Theodore Roosevelt's request to lead a division of troops to Europe in World War I?

137. How old was Abraham Lincoln in the print used for the engraving on the $5 bill?

138. Name the first President to talk on the radio.

139. Which President often woke up in the middle of the night and walked down to the White House Situation Room in his bathrobe?

ANSWERS

132. Chester Arthur

133. He was the only one wounded

134. Lyndon Johnson, from Judge Sarah Hughes

135. George H.W. Bush, who had joined the Navy the year before, on his 18th birthday

136. He said Roosevelt was "a great big boy"

137. 55

138. Woodrow Wilson

139. Lyndon Johnson, in search of the latest news from combat zones in Vietnam

140. Which former All-American football player was appointed to the Supreme Court by John Kennedy?

141. During Andrew Johnson's administration a large area of land was purchased by the U.S. What was it?

142. How much money did Lyndon Johnson bequeath to a former secretary, Mary Margaret Wiley Valenti?

143. How were George Washington and Sir Winston Churchill related?

144. What false charge against John Kennedy was retracted by ABC TV and columnist Drew Pearson?

145. The daughter of which President married the man who had been prosecuting officer at the trial of Aaron Burr?

146. How many slaves were in Virginia when Thomas Jefferson was elected Governor in 1779?

147. What startling disagreement was recorded by the two surgeons who conducted the autopsy on Abraham Lincoln?

ANSWERS

140. Byron White

141. Alaska—bought from Russia for $7.2 million

142. $3000

143. From a common 15th century ancestor, they were eighth cousins, six times removed

144. That John Kennedy had not authored the bestselling book, *Profiles in Courage*

145. James Monroe. His daughter, Eliza, married George Hay

146. 270,000

147. One said the bullet was behind the left eye while the other said it was behind the right eye

148. For which radio station in Des Moines, Iowa, did the young Ronald Reagan broadcast sports reports?

149. How long before Bill Clinton's birth did his biological father die in an auto accident?

150. Why was the reviewing stand empty when West Point cadets marched down Pennsylvania Avenue at President Taft's inauguration?

151. What was Vice President Agnew's reply when President Nixon asked what he should do about the Watergate tapes?

152. Name the two future Presidents who signed the U.S. Constitution.

153. Which two distinguished chroniclers of Presidential eras were classmates at Harvard?

154. What is *the football* which is always carried close to the President?

155. How many farms did George Washington maintain as separate units on his Mt. Vernon estate?

ANSWERS

148. WHO

149. Three months

150. Their train stalled in snow near Baltimore and when they got to Washington the parade was over—though they marched just the same

151. Agnew advised him to destroy them

152. George Washington and James Madison

153. Historian Arthur Schlesinger, Jr. and journalist Theodore White

154. The briefcase containing the codes which a President would utilize to launch nuclear weapons

155. Five

156. Why was Esther Cleveland's birth in the White House on September 9, 1893, one for the history books?

157. What was the Swiss family name of Herbert Hoover's forebears before it was Anglicized by his immigrant great-great-great grandfather?

158. What was President Nixon's reaction on learning that Dwight Eisenhower had just died?

159. Who were the last royal visitors entertained by Franklin Roosevelt before his death?

160. How many debates did Abraham Lincoln have with incumbent U.S. Senator Stephen Douglas in their 1858 Senate race?

161. How did former President Millard Fillmore escape his dread of having to kneel and kiss the Pope's hand or foot during a visit to Rome?

162. George H.W. Bush was very fond of sipping this beverage

ANSWERS

156. She was the first offspring of a President to be born in the White House

157. Huber

158. He wept

159. The Governor General of Canada, the Earl of Athlone, and his wife, Princess Alice

160. Seven

161. The Pope remained seated and offered neither his hand nor foot

162. Chinese tea

163. Andrew Jackson carried a bullet in his lung for the last four decades of his life. How did it get there?

164. Which President read the Bible from cover to cover annually?

165. Which President was charged by a Congressman with living so luxuriously that "your house glitters with all imaginable luxuries and gaudy ornaments"?

166. Name the Chief Executive whose spouse had been a fashion model and a professional dancer.

167. How did Richard Nixon meet his future wife, Pat Ryan?

168. Who was removed from the burial service for ex-President Andrew Jackson while screeching profanities?

169. In what manner was Sara Delano Roosevelt, mother of FDR, eccentric towards her dogs?

170. Where was President-elect Kennedy when told that his wife had just given birth to John, Jr.?

ANSWERS

163. In a duel fought in 1806 when he killed the man who had made insulting remarks about Jackson's wife, Rachel

164. John Quincy Adams

165. Martin Van Buren, 8th President

166. Gerald Ford

167. They both tried out for acting parts in *The Dark Tower*, a play performed by the Whittier Community Players in Whittier, Ca.

168. Jackson's pet parrot, Poll.

169. She mailed postcards to them

170. Aboard a DC-6 flying from West Palm Beach to Washington, D.C.

171. What rank did Harry Truman have in a field artillery unit in France during World War I?

172. How much did President Warren Harding owe his stockbrokers at the time of his death?

173. At what age was George Washington completely toothless?

174. Which father-figure President suffered from chronic constipation?

175. What California champagne was served aboard *Air Force One* during President Nixon's historic trip to China in 1972?

176. What were the measurements of Harry Truman's shirts?

177. How old was Thomas Jefferson at the time of his first inauguration?

178. What was Lyndon Johnson's first job in Washington, D.C.?

179. How fast was the Presidential limousine traveling when John Kennedy was shot?

ANSWERS

171. Captain

172. $180,000

173. 57

174. Abraham Lincoln

175. Schwansberg 1970

176. 15½" neck and 33" arm

177. 57

178. Private secretary (administrative aide) to Congressman Richard Kleberg (D-Texas)

179. 11.2 m.p.h.

180. Which President sent his daughter to a public school built originally for the children of freed slaves?

181. What names did the Marquis de Lafayette christen his son, in honor of his American friend?

182. What did Thomas Jefferson bequeath to his friend and successor as President, James Madison?

183. On what occasion were the famous paintings of *Washington Crossing the Delaware* and *Washington Reviewing the Army at Valley Forge,* reproduced as souvenir postage stamps?

184. What did President Wilson refer to as "My Boss"?

185. Why did Herbert Hoover pose for so many photographs with groups of visitors?

186. What was the cost of the casket in which the body of Abraham Lincoln was placed?

ANSWERS

180. Jimmy Carter

181. George Washington Lafayette

182. His gold-mounted walking staff of animal horn

183. The 1976 Bicentennial

184. His conscience

185. He did this instead of having to shake so many hands

186. $1500

187. What religious affiliation was shared by James Garfield, Lyndon Johnson and Ronald Reagan?

188. What was the name of Andrew Jackson's home, 12 miles from Nashville, Tennessee?

189. What was the name of the Scottie dog given by General Eisenhower to the woman with whom he was romantically linked during World War II?

190. This President met his wife when they were graduate students at Yale Law School.

191. Which of the following Chief Executives filled his glass with wine on his last night as President and told his guests: "This is the last time I shall drink your health as a public man"?
    a) George Washington
    b) Grover Cleveland
    c) Harry Truman
    d) Richard Nixon

192. Who changed the name of the Presidential retreat in the Maryland hills from *Shangri-la* to *Camp David?*

ANSWERS

187. They were all Disciples of Christ

188. The Hermitage

189. Telek

190. Bill Clinton

191. a) George Washington

192. Dwight Eisenhower, who named it after his grandson

193. Guess Bill Clinton's height.

194. How did Richard Nixon get his first view of the inside of the White House?

195. Which TV network did President Ford prefer to watch as results came in on the night he lost the election to Jimmy Carter?

196. When the Secretary of State hosts luncheons in his private suite at the State Department, a bas-relief of this President looks down the length of the table from its position on the wall. Whose likeness is it?

197. How did Andrew Jackson get the scar on his forehead?

198. While still in his twenties this future President was diagnosed by doctors as an epileptic. Who was he?

199. How long was the food table at the inaugural ball held in honor of President James Buchanan?

200. What happened to the Lincoln Continental limousine in which President Kennedy was shot?

ANSWERS

193. 6 ft. 2½"

194. In 1947 he attended a reception for freshmen Congressmen, given by President Truman

195. NBC

196. James Madison, by Giuseppe Ceracchi, 1794

197. A British officer struck Jackson, 13, with a sword when the boy refused to clean his boots

198. James Madison

199. 250 ft.

200. After extensive remodeling it was used by President Lyndon Johnson

201. Three months after eloping with Jefferson Davis, this daughter of a future President died. Name the father and daughter.

202. Which 19th century President likened Baltimore, Md. to "a swan sitting beautifully upon the water"?

203. Where did William Howard Taft begin the Presidential tradition of throwing out the first ball of the baseball season?

204. Which successful candidate for President refused to campaign across the nation, preferring instead to give short speeches from his porch in Canton, Ohio?

205. During which milestone in his life did Richard Nixon stand before the original Star Spangled Banner that inspired the words of the National Anthem?

206. How many slaves lived on the 1150-acre estate in Virginia where John Tyler lived after stepping down from the Presidency?

207. The mother of this Founding Father died in the year of the Declaration of Independence. Who was he?

ANSWERS

201. Zachary Taylor and his daughter, Sarah

202. John Tyler

203. At Griffith Stadium, Washington, D.C. (1910)

204. William McKinley, 25th President

205. At his inaugural ball, held in the Smithsonian Institution's Museum of American History, where the giant flag is hung

206. 30

207. Thomas Jefferson, son of Jane Randolph Jefferson

208. In which Washington, D.C. hotel was Millard Fillmore living when he was informed he had succeeded to the Presidency?

209. Did Ronald Reagan win more than 50 percent of the popular votes in the 1980 Presidential election?

210. What request did George Washington make of his secretary in the last words spoken from his death bed?

211. Who was the first Presidential spouse to graduate from college?

212. Whom did President Madison appoint as military commander of the Federal District after the British burned Washington in 1814?

213. Who was Abraham Lincoln's first love?

214. Guess the approximate cash value of the inheritance Theodore Roosevelt received on the death of his father.

215. Which Presidential assassin accidentally shot himself in the left elbow, while a Marine, when his loaded pistol fell out of his locker?

ANSWERS

208. The Willard

209. Yes. He won 50.75

210. Not to put his body in the vault until two days had passed

211. Lucy Hayes, wife of Rutherford Hayes

212. Former Secretary of State and later President, James Monroe

213. Ann Rutledge, who died aged 22 when Lincoln was 26

214. $125,000

215. Lee Harvey Oswald, in 1957

216. How many visits did Woodrow Wilson make to the home of Ellen Louise Axson before she accepted his marriage proposal?

217. When Gilbert Stuart said he wished he could have painted this woman when she was young, because he would then have had "a perfect Venus", which Presidential spouse was he referring to?

218. Which state has provided the most native-born sons as U.S. Presidents?

219. How long did Jimmy Carter negotiate at Camp David with Menahem Begin and Anwar Sadat?

220. How did Ronald Reagan get the nickname *Dutch?*

221. Who described the music of the Star Spangled Banner as "bad"?

222. What was the connection between James Bond and Lyndon Johnson?

223. Which Presidential challenger was awarded the Distinguished Flying Cross after flying B-24s in World War II?

ANSWERS

216. Eleven

217. Abigail Adams, wife of John Adams

218. Virginia (8)

219. 13 days

220. His father bestowed it on him at birth

221. Harry Truman

222. 007 was the code number given by the Secret Service to LBJ's brother, Sam Houston Johnson

223. George McGovern

224. How many men have become President because their predecessors were assassinated?

225. After helping end the Russo-Japanese War in 1905, Theodore Roosevelt was awarded which internationally renowned prize?

226. True or false: In 1945 President Truman offered to help General Eisenhower be President in 1948.

227. How far was Lee Harvey Oswald from his victim at the moment he shot President Kennedy in the head?

228. How many times did John Adams bow before King George III, following protocol, before presenting his diplomatic credentials?

229. Which President called the White House "the loneliest place in the world"?

230. What was Harry Truman's Washington, D.C. address immediately before he succeeded to the Presidency?

ANSWERS

224. Four

225. The Nobel Peace Prize

226. True, according to General Omar Bradley, who was present in the car in Berlin, Germany, when the offer was made

227. 265.3 ft.

228. Three times: on entering the room, halfway in the room, and when he stood before the King

229. William Howard Taft

230. An apartment at 4701 Connecticut Avenue, N.W.

231. Which American couple saved the Marquise de Lafayette from certain decapitation, the fate already suffered by her mother and grandmother during the French Revolution?

232. Which two Presidents were related to Richard Nixon?

233. Why did the citizens of Springfield, Illinois form an organization to protect the tomb of Abraham Lincoln?

234. Where did Dwight Eisenhower and Ulysses S. Grant study as young men?

235. On which occasion did Richard Nixon and John Kennedy share a train sleeping car compartment?

236. What was the first car owned by young marrieds, Jimmy and Rosalynn Carter?

237. Who made the final list of five persons from which Gerald Ford selected his Vice President?

238. What was the weight of the mass of cheese that Andrew Jackson made available for public consumption at the White House?

ANSWERS

231 James Monroe, U.S. Minister to France, and his wife, Elizabeth, after interceding with French officials

232. William Howard Taft was a 7th cousin twice removed and Herbert Hoover was an eighth cousin once removed

233. In 1876 an undercover agent learned of a plot to kidnap the corpse and exchange it for a jailed counterfeiter

234. They both attended the U.S. Military Academy

235. As freshmen Congressmen in 1947 they were returning from Pennsylvania, where they'd been invited to debate legislation affecting unions

236. A Studebaker

237. George Bush, Rogers Morton, Nelson Rockefeller, William Brock, John Rhodes

238. 1400 lbs.

239. Both Thomas Jefferson and Martin Van Buren sought recuperative power from the waters of this French spa. Where was it located?

240. What happened to all five children of Franklin and Eleanor Roosevelt after their marriages?

241. Are the greenhouse and adjoining servants' quarters at Mt. Vernon the original structures?

242. Guess the record number of hands President Coolidge said he shook in 34 minutes.

243. Which great love of George Washington remained loyal to the Crown and returned to England with her husband in 1773?

244. Where did Herbert Hoover regularly worship in Washington, D.C.?

245. Thomas Jefferson was 3rd President of the U.S. But he was also the first man to hold which Cabinet portfolio?

ANSWERS

239. Aix-les-Bains, southern France

240. They all got divorced

241. No. They were built after fire destroyed the originals in 1835

242. 1900

243. Sally Fairfax, wife of his neighbor and friend, George Fairfax

244. At Friends Meeting House, 2111 Florida Avenue, N.W.

245. Secretary of State

246. In which hotel did Ronald Reagan watch televised results of his overwhelming victories in the Presidential elections of 1980 and 1984?

247. What family tragedy prompted President Coolidge to write: "When he went, the power and glory of the Presidency went with him"?

248. What was so unusual about President Theodore Roosevelt insisting on going ahead with a speech in Milwaukee on October 14, 1912?

249. Though Ulysses S. Grant died almost penniless, his posthumously-published memoirs earned a fortune in royalties for his widow. How much was she paid?

250. Why did President Fillmore decline the offer of an honorary degree of Doctor of Civil Law from Oxford University?

251. Who dropped his first name, Thomas ("Tommy") only after graduating from Princeton?

252. Why did President McKinley often wheel his chair into position to face Lafayette Square?

ANSWERS

246. The Century Plaza Hotel, Los Angeles

247. The death of his youngest son, Calvin, Jr., 16, from blood poisoning

248. He had just been shot and the bullet was still in his chest

249. $450,000

250. He said he had not had a classical education and "no man should accept a degree he cannot read"

251. Woodrow Wilson

252. He said he was comforted by the view of St. John's Church spire

253. Name the famous poet who saw Abraham Lincoln riding through the streets almost daily, and wrote: "Only some curious stranger stops and gazes".

254. Who launched the carrier *John F. Kennedy?*

255. Which former President knew he had become addicted to cocaine?

256. What was so remarkable about 8-year-old Lyndon Johnson's school report card?

257. With the statement, "I feel as fit as a Bull Moose", this man gave the Progressive Party its unofficial name of the Bull Moose Party in 1912. Who was he?

258. What rank did Dwight Eisenhower have when he first met Mamie Doud, his future wife?

259. Who was the only President to graduate from the U.S. Naval Academy?

260. What was the highest percentage of popular votes cast which Franklin Roosevelt won during his four Presidential electoral victories?

ANSWERS

253. Walt Whitman

254. Caroline Kennedy

255. Ulysses S. Grant, under treatment for cancer of the throat

256. He got As in everything—arithmetic, geography, grammar, physiology, reading, spelling, writing—except for a C+ in deportment

257. Former President Theodore Roosevelt

258. Second Lieutenant

259. Jimmy Carter

260. 60.8 percent in 1936

261. What was Millard Fillmore doing when he had a stroke?

262. What was unique about the swearing-in ceremony of Calvin Coolidge?

263. What did Grover Cleveland wear in his mouth for the last 14 years of his life?

264. The *George Washington* ferried two illustrious Americans to Europe in connection with World War I. One was a President and the other would also be one. Who were they?

265. Which Founding Father was so nervous at his inauguration that those present could barely hear what he was saying?

266. How was Ronald Reagan dressed when Jimmy Carter telephoned to concede defeat in the 1980 election?

267. How long did it take Harry Truman to recognize the newly-proclaimed state of Israel?

268. How many people showed up for Abraham Lincoln's Gettysburg Address?

ANSWERS

261. Shaving

262. His father, a Notary Public and Justice of the Peace, administered the oath of office

263. An implanted rubber jawbone after the original cancerous bone was removed from the upper left region

264. Lt. Harry Truman sailed on it for France in 1918. Woodrow Wilson was aboard later for the Paris Peace Conference

265. George Washington

266. In a bath towel

267. 11 minutes

268. 15,000

269. How many Articles of Impeachment were adopted by the House of Representatives against President Andrew Johnson?

270. How many marchers took part in John Kennedy's inaugural parade?

271. Which high ranking officer traditionally lived in the Victorian mansion on the grounds of the U.S. Naval Observatory before it became the Vice President's residence in 1974?

272. British Prime Minister Winston Churchill wrote that he was impressed by this President's "precise, sparkling manner and obvious power of decision." Was he referring to
a) Franklin Roosevelt
b) Harry Truman
c) Dwight Eisenhower
d) John Kennedy

273. What did Julie Eisenhower give her father, Richard Nixon, immediately after he won the 1968 Presidential election?

ANSWERS

269. Eleven

270. 32,000

271. The Chief of Naval Operations

272. b) Harry Truman

273. The Great Seal of the United States, done
in crewelwork

274. Name the President who had the rare condition of being left-handed when he sat down and right-handed when he stood up.

275. Why did President Polk countermand an order by the Mayor of Washington to illuminate public buildings one night?

276. Who cradled the dying Franklin Roosevelt in her arms but was not mentioned by officials as being present at the scene?

277. What percentage of the votes cast in the Presidential election of 1960 were won respectively by John Kennedy and Richard Nixon?

278 Franklin Roosevelt vacationed for decades on Campobello Island, just across the Canadian border in New Brunswick. How did he get to own the cottage on it?

279. What diplomatic post did John Quincy Adams hold during his father's Presidency?

280. What did Harry Truman eat after he was sworn in as President?

ANSWERS

274. Gerald Ford

275. He said it would create a fire hazard

276. Lucy (Mercer) Rutherfurd, with whom he was romantically linked for many years

277. 49.7 percent for Kennedy; 49.6 percent for Nixon

278. It was a wedding present

279. Minister to Prussia

280. A roast beef sandwich back at his neighbor's apartment on Connecticut Avenue, Washington, D.C.

281. Where is the only statue of George Washington executed from life?

282. Why were James Monroe's remains removed from a New York City cemetery to Hollywood Cemetery in Richmond, Va., 27 years after his death?

283. What three similarities were conspicuous in the assassinations of Abraham Lincoln and John Kennedy?

284. Who was the first President born after U.S. independence?

285. How long had Thomas Jefferson been a widower when he became President?

286. Why did President Cleveland's widow make the record books when she married five years after his death?

287. Whom did Ronald Reagan address at the Washington Hilton Hotel immediately before he was shot?

288. What were the average yearly expenses of John Adams while he was Minister Plenipotentiary in Paris?

ANSWERS

281. In the Rotunda of the Capitol in Richmond, Va.

282. On the centenary of his birth Virginia legislators voted funds for the reinterment because they wanted native son Presidents buried in Virginia

283. Both were shot in the back of the head, on a Friday, as they sat next to their wives

284. Martin Van Buren (1782)

285. 19 years

286. She was the first Presidential spouse to remarry

287. Leaders of the Building & Construction Trades Department of the AFL-CIO

288. $6000

289. Which President tumbled down a plane ramp on arrival in Salzburg, Austria?

290. Where did Richard Nixon's top lieutenants, Bob Haldeman and John Ehrlichman, know each other from?

291. What grim reminder of the Revolutionary War remained in the body of James Monroe for the rest of his life?

292. Of the 820 midshipmen in Jimmy Carter's class at the Naval Academy, Annapolis, where did he stand?

293. Why was Sergeant Dwight Eisenhower demoted to Private while a cadet at West Point?

294. Who was the only California-born President?

295. Name the incumbent President who made his wife and doctor promise to keep secret from the public his cerebral thrombosis.

296. Name the President who said, "James, will you please put out the light," then died in his sleep.

ANSWERS

289. Gerald Ford

290. They were undergraduates together at the University of California, Los Angeles

291. A bullet in his left shoulder, fired during the battle for Trenton

292. 59th

293. For whirling around a dance floor in violation of an earlier warning not to repeat it

294. Richard Nixon

295. Woodrow Wilson

296. Theodore Roosevelt

297. What were the last words uttered by Calvin Coolidge?

298. Why did Andrew Jackson flee the White House on inauguration day 1829?

299. To whom was Lyndon Johnson referring when he came out of the first Kennedy Cabinet meeting and said: "That man with the stacomb in his hair is the best of the lot"?

300. How many Presidents did Chief Justice William Howard Taft, himself a former President, swear into office?

301. Name the first Quaker President.

302. During whose administration was California admitted to the Union as the 31st state?

303. As Commander in Chief, George Washington's mess kit accompanied him throughout the Revolutionary War. What was it made of?

ANSWERS

297. "Good morning, Robert"

298. To escape the mobs swarming in for food and liquor, and also to shake his hand

299. Secretary of Defense Robert McNamara

300. Two: Calvin Coolidge (at the public ceremony) and Herbert Hoover

301. Herbert Hoover

302. Millard Fillmore's

303. It was a wooden chest covered with leather and lined with green wool

304. Among the doctors attending the dying President Kennedy was one who had qualified outside the English-speaking world. Where did he qualify?

305. Why did Thomas Jefferson take his daughter, Martha, out of her French convent school?

306. Why is August 27 a legal holiday in Texas?

307. What date was of shared significance to Ronald Reagan and Queen Elizabeth 11 of England?

308. While at Yale, this future President was turned off by what he called its "intellectual snobbery"

309. When George Washington's great-grandfather sailed from England to Virginia, what rank did he have among the crew?

310. Who appointed George H.W. Bush to head the CIA?

311. What time of the day did President John Quincy Adams normally get up and then retire to bed at night?

ANSWERS

304 Dr. Fouad Bashour graduated at the University of Beirut School of Medicine in Lebanon.

305. Because she said she wanted to be a nun

306. It is the anniversary of President Lyndon Johnson's birthday

307. February 6th. Reagan was born on this date in 1911. On this day, in 1952, Princess Elizabeth became Queen on the death of her father

308. George W. Bush

309. Ship's mate

310. President Ford

311. He frequently rose before 4 a.m. and went to bed between 11 p.m. and midnight

312. Who was the first woman to give birth in the White House?

313. How many miles did Abraham Lincoln's funeral train travel on its cross-state journey from the Capital to Springfield, Illinois?

314. What tragedy struck the family of Robert Lincoln, son of Abraham Lincoln, while he was U.S. Minister to England?

315. Why was the air-raid alarm sounded on November 3, 1948 in Independence, Missouri?

316. How much silverware was missing after a buffet lunch for 1800 persons following Franklin Roosevelt's fourth inauguration?

317. Who was with Lyndon Johnson when he died at his ranch?

318. How old was John Kennedy when he received a $1 million trust fund from his father?

319. Name the Irish-born woman who was romantically linked with Dwight Eisenhower during World War II.

ANSWERS

312. Martha "Patsy" Randolph—Thomas Jefferson's daughter

313. 1662 miles

314. His 16-year-old only son died while at school in France

315. In celebration of citizen Harry Truman's unexpected reelection to the Presidency

316. Only one spoon

317. No one

318. 21

319. Kay Summersby

320. Guess the favorite relish of Arkansas-born Bill Clinton.

321. To whom did Jimmy Carter confess that he had not always done his best at the Naval Academy, Annapolis?

322. With what words did Ronald Reagan dedicate his autobiography, first published in 1965 under the title, *Where's the Rest of Me?*

323. Name the President who took cold baths and swam against the Potomac River current to keep fit.

324. What was one of President Johnson's first acts on learning of the assassination of Robert Kennedy?

325. What did octogenarian former President James Madison wear on his head in his final years?

326. Name the wine most regularly served by George Washington to his guests.

327. What priceless gift did King Ibn Saud of Saudi Arabia give President Truman?

ANSWERS

320. Watermelon rind pickle

321. Captain (later Admiral) Hyman Rickover

322. *To Nancy With Love*

323. John Quincy Adams

324. He ordered Secret Service protection for the victim's only surviving brother, Edward Kennedy

325. A white knitted cap

326. Madeira

327. A golden scimitar, its handle studded with jewels

328. What did Richard Nixon customarily give his wife and daughters for Christmas?

329. Which President appointed the most Supreme Court Justices?

330. Name the avowed segregationist who defeated Jimmy Carter in the 1966 Georgia gubernatorial race.

331. What did Thomas Jefferson believe to be the best form of exercise?

332. What public ceremony did Gerald Ford perform just before President Nixon told him he was resigning?

333. How did President Johnson physically hurt Israeli Foreign Minister Abba Eban on the eve of the Six Day War?

334. What was President Kennedy's favorite room in the White House?

335. How heavy was Franklin Roosevelt at birth?

336. Before his election to the Presidency this man taught briefly at the Harvard Business School.

ANSWERS

328. Jewelry

329. George Washington (10)

330. Lester Maddox

331. Walking

332. He presented Medals of Honor to families of servicemen killed in Vietnam

333. He shook Eban's hand so forcefully that the Israeli felt he would never regain the use of it

334. The Green Room

335. 10 lbs.

336. Herbert Hoover

337. How old was George H.W. Bush when shot down in World War 11 by the Japanese?

338. Whose favorite day-time clothes included a dark suit with pantaloons to his knees, white-topped boots and a dark beaver hat?

339. What was the population of the U.S. when Andrew Jackson's term of office was up in 1837?

340. How much money did Frank Sinatra loan Spiro Agnew for living expenses and to pay off fines and the IRS soon after the Vice President's resignation?

341. How many peach trees did Thomas Jefferson plant in the month of December 1795 at Monticello?

342. What gruesome story did Franklin Roosevelt relate the day six Nazi saboteurs were electrocuted in Washington, D.C.?

343. Name the Ohio newspaper edited by Warren Harding before his election to the Presidency

ANSWERS

337. 20 years old

338. James Monroe

339. 15.9 million

340. $230,000

341. 1151

342. A tale of a barber killing his customers and delivering them as meat to a butcher

343. The Marion *Star*

344. On what momentous day did John, son of Dwight Eisenhower, graduate from West Point?

345. From where did Harry Truman make the decision to defend South Korea after the invasion by North Koreans?

346. What instructions did George Washington leave in his will regarding his slaves?

347. Who vomited in President Carter's bathroom after learning that the mission to rescue hostages in Iran had failed?

348. Why did President Nixon demonstrably offer a handshake on first meeting Chinese Premier Chou En-lai?

349. Why did Ulysses S. Grant sleep for several months in an easy chair?

350. What were former President John Adams' last words on his deathbed?

351. What was the D.C. license number of President Calvin Coolidge's official car?

ANSWERS

344. June 6, 1944, the day the allies landed in Europe, with his father in overall command

345. Blair House, Washington, D.C.

346. He wanted them all freed after the death of his wife, Martha

347. White House Chief of Staff, Hamilton Jordan

348. Because the Premier had been snubbed 18 years earlier when a Secretary of State had declined to shake his hand

349. To prevent him from choking in the advanced stage of cancer of the throat

350. ''Thomas Jefferson survives''—not knowing that Jefferson had died earlier that same afternoon

351. 100

352. How many hours of sleep did James Madison allow himself for months on end while an undergraduate at Princeton?

353. Dr. Charles Leale, the first doctor to reach Abraham Lincoln seconds after he was shot, died in 1932 aged 90. What memento of the assassination did he keep all those years?

354. How many words make up the oath/affirmation of office that the incoming President must recite before assuming office?

355. Why were the remains of President William Henry Harrison removed three months after burial in Congressional Cemetery, Washington, D.C.?

356. Why did John Tyler return a lot of his mail unopened?

357. How many press conferences did Gerald Ford have while Vice President?

358. When did John Kennedy do the research for his Pulitzer prizewinning book, *Profiles in Courage*?

ANSWERS

352. Three hours a night

353. His blood-stained cuffs

354. 35

355. His family requested removal of his remains to North Bend, Ohio

356. He objected to mail being addressed to *The Acting President*, the title many officials wanted to use when he became the first Vice President to succeed a man who died in office

357. 55

358. During hospitalization and convalescence after a spinal operation

359. Which old soldier President was known as *Old Rough & Ready* by his troops?

360. Why was there no inaugural ball at Woodrow Wilson's first inauguration?

361. What is the minimum age requirement for anyone wanting to be a candidate for President?

362. How many ballots were required at the Democratic National Convention in 1924 before John William Davis of West Virginia won the Presidential nomination?

363. How much did Theodore Roosevelt make on his book, *African Game Trails*?

364. Which President began Volume 2 of his memoirs with the words: "Being a President is like riding a tiger"?

365. What was President Eisenhower's favorite form of relaxation, after golf?

366. Name the singer who spoke out against U.S. policy in Vietnam during a White House luncheon for women.

ANSWERS

359. Zachary Taylor, 12th President

360. His first wife, Ellen, said an inauguration was a dedication and not a social event

361. 35 years old

362. 103

363. A guaranteed fee of $50,000 plus about $40,000 net

364. Harry Truman

365. Landscape painting

366. Eartha Kitt

367. How many shots did President Garfield's assassin fire from his revolver?

368. From what date were President Nixon's office conversations bugged and telephones tapped?

369. John Tyler holds the record for the President who fathered the most children. How many offspring did he have?

370. Besides Bill Clinton, which other 20th century Presidents defeated incumbents?

371. Something about the signature of James Buchanan makes it perhaps the most conspicuous of all Presidential handwriting. Guess what it is.

372. Why were the remains of Lou Hoover reburied 20 years after her death?

373. How did John Kennedy save one of his crewmen when their PT-109 torpedo boat was sliced in two by a Japanese destroyer?

ANSWERS

367. Two

368. Spring 1971

369. 8 sons and 7 daughters

370. Woodrow Wilson, Franklin Roosevelt, Jimmy Carter and Ronald Reagan

371. He had, perhaps, the neatest handwriting

372. President Hoover died two decades after his wife and wanted her remains taken from California and reburied next to his in Iowa

373. He swam three miles, hauling the man by clasping the life-belt strap in his teeth

374. Which President failed in his attempt to pack the Supreme Court with Justices who would have been sympathetic to his program?

375. Who resigned from the Ford administration just before the President pardoned Nixon?

376. How is the office of Vice President filled when a vacancy occurs?

377. Where was George Washington's first inauguration held?

378. In what year was the last portrait of George Washington painted from life?

379. Dr. Loyal Davis, the surgeon who adopted Nancy Reagan, wrote a manuscript on the life of a doctor who cared for which wounded President?

380. By what time in the morning was President Lyndon Johnson already regularly on the telephone?

381. When was the birthplace of George Washington at Popes Creek Plantation, Va., completely destroyed by fire?

ANSWERS

374. Franklin Roosevelt

375. Presidential Press Secretary Jerald terHorst

376. The President nominates a Vice President but confirmation is required by a majority vote of both houses of Congress

377. Federal Hall, Wall Street, New York City

378. 1798—the year before Washington's death—by the French artist Charles St. Mamin

379. Theodore Roosevelt

380. Before his 7:30–8:00 a.m. breakfast

381. Christmas Day 1779

382. Where is the Herbert Hoover Presidential library?

383. What advice did the Supreme Court Justices give James Monroe when his inauguration fell on a Sunday?

384. During whose administration did the Senate, for the first time in history, reject a President's nominee for a Cabinet post?

385. Who declined President-elect Kennedy's offers to be either Secretary of Defense, State or Treasury?

386. What was the area of Virginia when Thomas Jefferson was Governor?

387. How did President Andrew Johnson make history after his term was up?

388. Which former President described Rock 'n Roll music as "this damn noise they play today"?

389. What did George Washington wear for his first inauguration?

390. How tall was Jimmy Carter?

ANSWERS

382. In West Branch, Iowa, his birthplace

383. They suggested postponing it until Monday

384. Andrew Jackson's nominee for Secretary of the Treasury, Roger Taney, was rejected

385. Robert Lovett, Secretary of Defense under Harry Truman

386. Over 60,000 sq. miles, embracing Virginia, West Virginia, Kentucky and parts of Illinois, Ohio and Indiana

387. He became the only ex-Chief Executive elected to the U.S. Senate

388. Harry Truman

389. A brown cloth suit, white silk stockings and silver-buckled shoes

390. 5 ft. 9½ in.

391. Which two former Presidents, who had snubbed each other for years, motored in the same car for the burial of John Kennedy?

392. Why did General Eisenhower drink champagne during a pre-dawn breakfast on Washington's Birthday, 1951?

393. On what occasion did three former Presidents gather together with the incumbent President at the White House?

394. During his honeymoon in Europe, Franklin Roosevelt described this location as more wonderful than he had imagined. Where was he?

395. What was macabre about the only two meetings President Johnson had with French President Charles de Gaulle?

396. How many people gathered at the White House grounds for Herbert Hoover's open-house New Year reception in 1930?

397. How did Warren Harding enjoy relaxing?

398. Who was the first President to appear on television?

ANSWERS

391. Harry Truman and Dwight Eisenhower

392. Local officials feted him on arrival in France as the new commander of NATO forces

393. President Reagan invited Nixon, Ford and Carter prior to the latter three flying to Anwar Sadat's funeral

394. In Venice, Italy

395. They met only at the funerals of John Kennedy and West German Chancellor Konrad Adenauer

396. About 9,000

397. By playing poker

398. Franklin Roosevelt (1939)

399. What was the speed of the assassin's bullet which exited from President Kennedy's neck?

400. Which states did Franklin Roosevelt fail to carry when Kansas Governor Alf Landon challenged him in 1936?

401. Why did Vice President Thomas Jefferson reluctantly follow John Adams out of Congress Hall after the latter had been sworn in as President?

402. Which First Lady began the custom of serving food when she and the President gave their staff Christmas presents?

403. Just before graduating in law, this future President tried for a job with the FBI but got no reply. Who was he?

404. What were the limits of Gerald Ford's ambitions before he became President?

405. What was Richard Nixon's annual income from the California law firm he joined after defeat in the 1960 Presidential race?

ANSWERS

399. 1772 to 1779 ft. per second

400. Maine and Vermont

401. Jefferson wanted retiring President George Washington to have the honor of following the President, but Washington insisted the Veep abide by protocol

402. Mamie Eisenhower

403. Richard Nixon

404. He wanted to be Speaker of the House of Representatives

405. $100,000

406. For what historic vote were one paralyzed and another very ill Senator brought into the U.S. Senate chamber?

407. Why was an operation on President Cleveland carried out in secrecy aboard a yacht on Manhattan's East River?

408. Who was given the Secret Service code name of *Rawhide?*

409. Who told U.S. Minister to England, John Adams, that he always rose at 5 a.m. and made his own fire?

410. Where was Gerald Ford sworn in as 38th President?

411. Who sang for John Kennedy when he was in Vienna, Austria for a summit meeting with Soviet leader Nikita Khrushchev?

412. In what circumstances did President John Quincy Adams' eldest son, George, drown in Long Island Sound?

413. How many Governors of Georgia had there been before Jimmy Carter's election to that office?

ANSWERS

406. To vote in the impeachment trial of President Andrew Johnson

407. The U.S. was going through a financial crisis, which might have worsened by news of this threat to the President's life

408. Ronald Reagan

409. King George III

410. In the East Room of the White House

411. The Vienna Boys' Choir

412. George and his brother, John, both wooed the same woman. When John married her, George took to the bottle and was drunk when he fell overboard

413 75

414. Aboard which British cruiser did Harry Truman meet King George VI after the Potsdam conference?

415. When George Wallace ran for President in 1968 he won 13.5 percent of the popular votes. How many votes did he get?

416. Who was present as each of three Presidents lay mortally wounded by assassins' bullets?

417. To whom did Jimmy Carter dedicate his book, *Why Not The Best?*

418. Which future President testified before the House Un-American Activities Committee when Congressman Richard Nixon was a committee member?

419. Who bought John Kennedy's Georgetown home after his election to the Presidency?

420. During William McKinley's administration the U.S.A. acquired its first possessions abroad. Name them.

421. Where did Dwight Eisenhower die?

ANSWERS

414. HMS *Renown*

415. 9,906,473

416. Robert Lincoln, son of Abraham Lincoln, was by his dying father's bedside. He witnessed the shooting of President Garfield in Washington, D.C. and was a guest at the Exposition in Buffalo, N.Y. where President McKinley was shot

417. His mother, Lillian, and his wife, Rosalynn

418. Ronald Reagan, when President of the Screen Actors Guild, in 1947

419. Mr. and Mrs. Perry Ausbrook

420. The Philippines, Puerto Rico, Guam

421. In Walter Reed Hospital, Washington, D.C.

422. The only mention this President made of his mother in his autobiography were the dates of her birth, marriage and death. Name the President.

423. The Czar of Russia was so complimentary of this future President that he said he hoped the U.S. would send another Minister like him. Who was the American?

424. How much money did Lyndon Johnson bequeath to his brother, Sam Houston Johnson?

425. Why did Abraham Lincoln cry in the White House on a February night in 1864?

426. What was the name of the cruiser bringing Harry Truman across the Atlantic as the atomic bomb was dropped on Hiroshima?

427. Name the four incumbent Vice Presidents who won election to the Presidency.

428. Where did President Nixon attend his final campaign rally as a political candidate?

ANSWERS

422. Thomas Jefferson

423. James Buchanan

424. $5,000

425. The adjoining stables burned down and took the lives of his horses and the ponies of his son, Tad, and his late son, Willie

426. USS *Augusta*

427. John Adams, Thomas Jefferson, Martin Van Buren, George H.W. Bush

428. Ontario, California (November 1972)

429. Which biblical passage did Jimmy Carter quote in his inaugural address?

430. Who nominated George Washington as Commander in Chief of the Continental Army?

431. Why was the inauguration of William Howard Taft moved from the Capitol steps to the Senate chamber?

432. What is so significant about the book, *King Arthur's Knights,* in the nursery of the Brookline, Mass. home where John Kennedy was born?

433. For what purpose did President Truman instruct Army Chief of Staff Dwight Eisenhower to relay a secret message to General George Marshall in 1946?

434. How did Lyndon Johnson's wife, Claudia, get the name *Lady Bird*?

435. How old was Richard Nixon when first elected to the House of Representatives?

436. This President was allergic to beef, milk, house dust, mold spores, weed & grass pollens and cat dander.

ANSWERS

429. Micah 6:8

430. John Adams (later President)

431. Because of a heavy snowstorm

432. It was one of his favorite childhood books

433. To ask Marshall if he would agree to be Secretary of State

434. A nurse said she was ''pretty as a Lady Bird''

435. 33

436. Bill Clinton

437. Until what date will certain letters from President Harding to Mrs. Carrie Phillips be withheld from the public by the Library of Congress?

438. In what unusual circumstances did Thomas Jefferson's younger sister, Elizabeth, 29, die?

439. Which member of the President's Commission on the Assassination of President Kennedy later became President himself?

440. Whom did Ronald Reagan choose as his prospective running mate in his quest for his party's Presidential nomination in 1976?

441. Where did Richard Nixon dine the night he told a surprised nation that he would visit the People's Republic of China for the first time?

442. A great lover of trees, George Washington wrote often in his diaries about planting and observing them. About how many words did he write on the subject of trees between 1760–1788?

ANSWERS

437. 2014

438. She died of exposure after hiding in a ditch for two days during an earthquake at Shadwell, Va.

439. Gerald Ford

440. Senator Richard Schweiker (R-Pa.)

441. Perino's Restaurant in Los Angeles

442. More than 10,000 words

443. Which Republican President declared there was "no right to strike against the public safety by anybody, anywhere, anytime"?

444. How many Presidents were survived by both their parents?

445. Which President had been chosen the outstanding member of his class and class valedictorian at the age of 13?

446. Why was Martin Van Buren the first President to have more than one inaugural ball?

447. What event from his youth did Franklin Roosevelt regard as one of the greatest disappointments in his life?

448. Was James Buchanan ever engaged, even though he was the only President to remain a lifelong bachelor?

449. At what hour and date did President Lyndon Johnson tell the American people that he had ordered the first bombing raid against North Vietnam?

ANSWERS

443. Calvin Coolidge

444. Only one—John Kennedy

445. Richard Nixon

446. The demand for tickets necessitated organizing more than one ball

447. His failure to be accepted into Porcellian, Harvard University's most exclusive club

448. Yes, but his fiancée broke it off

449. 11:36 p.m. EST, August 4, 1964

450. In which plush White House room did Calvin Coolidge keep his dog's drinking bowl?

451. What made Virginia statesman, General Henry Wise, fume: "The man does not live, and never did live, who saw Washington without his shirt!"?

452. How much did John Kennedy pay for his Georgetown home in 1957 and what did he get for it four years later, after $20,000 worth of improvements?

453. At which university did William Howard Taft teach law after his term as President?

454. Why did President Hoover's daughter-in-law, Margaret, and her three children live in the White House?

455. True or false: Frank Sinatra supported Richard Nixon for President in 1960.

456. How many telephones are installed in the nuclear-powered aircraft carrier, *Theodore Roosevelt*?

457. What right do all of Thomas Jefferson's descendents have?

ANSWERS

450. The State Dining Room

451. The arrival in the capital of the statue of George Washington, showing him stripped to the waist

452. He paid $78,000 and got $105,000

453. Yale

454. Her husband, the President's son, was hospitalized for a year with tuberculosis

455. False. He supported John Kennedy

456. More than 2,000

457. To be buried in the family graveyard at Monticello, Va.

458. How was Andrew Jackson's home in Tennessee destroyed in 1834 while he was in the White House?

459. Who was the first daughter of a President to be married in the White House?

460. Who becomes President if a candidate wins the election but dies before inauguration day?

461. What were Woodrow Wilson's last words?

462. An assassin's bullets missed their mark but mortally wounded the Mayor of Chicago. Who was the lucky escapee?

463. What location did Ronald Reagan choose to announce his candidacy for the governorship of California in 1966?

464. As a student at Duke University, North Carolina, this future President was elected president of the student bar association. Who was he?

465. How old was Martha Ellen Truman, mother of President Truman, when she died during his first term, in 1947?

ANSWERS

458. A spark from the chimney set it alight

459. Maria Hester Monroe, daughter of James Monroe (1820)

460. The deceased's running mate

461. "I am ready"

462. President-elect Franklin Roosevelt (1933)

463. The Statler-Hilton Hotel, Los Angeles

464. Richard Nixon

465. 94

466. How many inaugural parties did Jimmy and Rosalynn Carter attend on his first night as President?

467. Which President began his term by refusing to sign a document he had not read, but by his fourth year asked simply where he was meant to sign?

468. Where was Theodore Roosevelt married?

469. When former Israeli Defense Minister Ezer Weizman wrote that "...no American President has ever helped Israel as much as....," who was he referring to?

470. Which top aide to President Nixon secretly wired his own White House office so he could tape conversations?

471. In Thomas Jefferson's words, this period of life was considered the "arch of matrimonial happiness." What was it?

472. Who commuted the life imprisonment sentence on a Puerto Rican who had tried to assassinate an earlier President?

ANSWERS

466. Eleven

467. Abraham Lincoln

468. In St. George's Church in London's fashionable Hanover Square

469 Jimmy Carter

470. Domestic Affairs adviser, John Ehrlichman

471. Parenthood

472. Jimmy Carter commuted the sentence on a man who'd tried to kill Harry Truman

473. Which future President coached boxing and football at Yale University, where he graduated in law?

474. Who was the first person to address Lyndon Johnson as "Mr. President"?

475. Who served as Vice President in both of George Washington's administrations?

476. Name the first President to review the inaugural parade from a heated reviewing stand.

477. Who wrote that the FBI was "dabbling in sex life scandals and plain blackmail when they should be catching criminals"?

478. Name the President's widow who died a block from the White House while listening to a reading from the Bible.

479. Where was Thomas Jefferson's mother born?

480. Which former Vice President received a birthday call from President Kennedy the day JFK was shot?

ANSWERS

473. Gerald Ford

474. Assistant Presidential Press Secretary Malcolm Kilduff, about 1:30 p.m. on November 22, 1963, said: "Mr. President, I have to announce the death of President Kennedy"

475. John Adams, second President of the U.S.

476. Lyndon Johnson

477. Harry Truman

478. Dolley Madison

479. London, England

480. John Nance Garner

481. Which retired President found Norway "as funny a kingdom as was ever imagined outside *opera bouffe*"?

482. In whose administration did the First Lady's chief of staff have the same salary as the President's chief of staff?

483. What percentage of the votes cast in the Presidential election of 1864 went to Abraham Lincoln?

484. Who stabbed four cougars to death with a hunting knife to save his pack of hunting dogs further injury?

485. This Chief Justice of the Supreme Court had previously been High Commissioner to the Philippines, then U.S. President. Who was he?

486. Which monarch gave the United States a desk which was later used by John Kennedy in the Oval Office?

487. Name the future President who defied protocol by personally inviting a Pakistani camel driver to the United States.

ANSWERS

481. Theodore Roosevelt

482. Jimmy Carter's

483. 55.09 percent

484. Vice President-elect Theodore Roosevelt, during a trip to Colorado

485. William Howard Taft

486. Britain's Queen Victoria

487. Lyndon Johnson, while Vice President, without going through any formalities

488. How much older than his wife was John Kennedy?

489. Why did Lyndon Johnson explode in rage the night of his electoral victory against Barry Goldwater?

490. Which chief executive eagerly read the James Bond books by Ian Fleming?

491. What was the nickname of President Reagan's older brother, Neil?

492. Who was in constitutional line to succeed President Nixon after Vice President Agnew's resignation, but before the appointment of Gerald Ford as his replacement?

493. How did Pennsylvania Congressmen, opposed to Vice President John Adams' lobbying for the necessity of titles, derisively refer to him?

494. What did President Johnson give his daughter, Luci, on her graduation from National Cathedral School?

ANSWERS

488. 12 years

489. Reporters spoiled his hopes for a surprise appearance at the Austin, Texas Civic Center, by correctly guessing his movements

490. John Kennedy

491. Moon

492. House Speaker Carl Albert (D-Oklahoma)

493. *His Rotundity*

494. A Corvette Sting-Ray auto

495. Why did Thomas Jefferson and his bride of a few hours have to abandon their carriage on the way to Monticello?

496. Why did Vice President Agnew meet alone in the Oval Office with President Nixon on October 9, 1973?

497. Which great American was referred to when the visiting Lieutenant-General of France wrote: ''In Europe he would hold a distinguished rank among men of letters''?

498. What was the name of the Presidential train in which Harry Truman whistle-stopped during his 1948 re-election campaign?

499. Which world statesman did Jimmy Carter admit he admired more than any other leader?

500. Whose christening did President Kennedy attend as godfather, in Westminster Cathedral, London?

501. Who wrote the bestselling book, *Crusade in Europe*?

ANSWERS

495. Snow piled up to more than two feet deep

496. To tell the President that he would resign the Vice Presidency the following day

497. Thomas Jefferson

498. *Ferdinand Magellan*

499. Egyptian President Anwar Sadat

500. Anna Christina Radziwill, daughter of his wife's sister, Lee

501. Dwight Eisenhower

502. When White House staff scrambled to find a Bible for Harry Truman's swearing-in ceremony, which one did they locate?

503. Franklin Roosevelt was a second cousin seven times removed of which British monarch?

504. Only three days before his death Andrew Jackson again tried to get a loan to cover the debts of this wayward relative. Who was he?

505. What movie was shown at the Kennedy compound in Hyannisport the day John Kennedy was elected President?

506. Upon which historic desk did President Nixon certify the 26th Amendment, granting the vote to 18-year-olds?

507. Which President's ancestors fled Switzerland's religious persecution in the 17th century?

508. In what ceremonial gear did the normally modestly dressed John Adams dress for his inauguration?

ANSWERS

502. One that the Gideons had presented for the guest rooms

503. Queen Elizabeth II

504. His adopted son, Andrew Jackson, Jr.

505. *Butterfield 8*

506. The same desk upon which Thomas Jefferson is believed to have drafted the Declaration of Independence

507. Herbert Hoover's

508. A pearl-colored broadcloth suit, cockade and sword

509. By what nickname was Ulysses S. Grant known in his youth?

510. How many children did Jimmy Carter have?

511. Who wrote to congratulate Richard Nixon on being "an ideal selection" as Eisenhower's running mate in 1952?

512. How old was Gerald Ford when his mother told him that her second husband was not his real father?

513. Who was the first Vice President to move into the Veep's new official residence at the U.S. Naval Observatory grounds in Washington, D.C.?

514. Who was the only President sworn into office aboard an aircraft?

515. Why did Theodore Roosevelt's hopes for an audience with the Pope come to nothing?

516. What wedding present did Nancy and Ronald Reagan give Prince Charles and his bride, Diana?

ANSWERS

509. *Useless* Grant

510. Three sons and one daughter

511. Fellow Congressman John Kennedy

512. 12 or 13

513. Walter Mondale

514. Lyndon Johnson

515. He refused to knuckle under to the Pontiff's condition that Roosevelt not meet with Methodist missionaries in Rome

516. A Steuben glass bowl

517. What scholastic achievement made Bill Clinton unique among his presidential predecessors?

518. By what affectionate name did Harry Truman call his daughter, Margaret?

519. Why did Franklin Roosevelt withdraw to the family quarters in the White House almost immediately after his fourth inauguration?

520. Who administered the oath of office to George Washington at his second inauguration?

521. What location did President Nixon choose to fire his top lieutenants, Bob Haldeman and John Ehrlichman, during the Watergate scandal?

522. When did the athletic President Ford take his last swim in the White House pool?

523. For what occasion did President Kennedy sit with former Presidents Eisenhower and Truman?

ANSWERS

517. He was the only Rhodes Scholar

518. "My Baby"

519. To escape shaking hands with 1805 invitees to a buffet lunch

520. Supreme Court Justice William Cushing

521. Camp David, Md.

522. The day before his term was up

523. At the funeral of House Speaker Sam Rayburn

524. What happened to the Buckeye tree planted by Edward, Prince of Wales, near George Washington's tomb?

525. On what national holiday did Rosalynn Smith change her mind and accept Jimmy Carter's proposal of marriage?

526. When did Franklin Roosevelt start calling his wife by the nickname *Babs*?

527. Woodrow Wilson was the first President since John Adams to revive this practice, now accepted as part and parcel of visible American democracy.

528. Only when this man was elected President was it confirmed that he had been born in Denison, Texas. Who was he?

529. Why did First Lady Lou Hoover hang linen in the East Room of the White House?

530. How much did President Polk donate in the fundraiser for a statue of former President Andrew Jackson?

531. When Lyndon Johnson gave up hard liquor early in his Presidency, what did he drink instead?

ANSWERS

524. It died

525. Washington's Birthday

526. On their honeymoon

527. Addressing joint sessions of Congress

528. Dwight Eisenhower

529. They were gifts from a linen shower for her secretary

530. The maximum allowable of $100

531. Tea, Tab and Fresca

532. Whose administration was so wracked by corruption that even his Secretary of the Interior was jailed for bribery?

533. What instructions for his grave did Harry Truman suggest in a codicil added to his last Will?

534. Name the Democrat who won 53.6 percent of the California gubernatorial vote in 1962 to defeat Richard Nixon.

535. When Dwight Eisenhower was made a Freeman of the City of London what treasured memento was he given?

536. From which book did Gerald Ford lift a quote for the title of his autobiography?

537. Who was the first American President to address the Russians on their own TV?

538. Name the President whose statue stands outside the City Hall in Buffalo, N.Y.

539. Who was the first Chief Executive to leave the U.S.A. during wartime?

ANSWERS

532. Warren Harding's

533. The wording on the *flat* slab, which included only the dates of his birth, marriage, birth of his daughter, and public offices he held

534. Edmund G. "Pat" Brown

535. A Crusader-type sword

536. The Bible. *A Time to Heal* is from Ecclesiastes 3:3

537. Richard Nixon, in 1972

538. Millard Fillmore

539. Franklin Roosevelt, for a meeting with Winston Churchill in Casablanca, 1943

540. A portrait of which President hung on the wall close to Harry Truman's bed in the White House?

541. At the time Lyndon Johnson became President how much did the *Washington Post* estimate the value of the Johnson radio and TV holdings?

542. Who confessed to being the Errol Flynn of the B-movies?

543. What specifications did Thomas Jefferson give for his custom-designed spectacles?

544. Before she married Jimmy Carter, how had Rosalynn Smith distinguished herself at Plains High School?

545. Why did U.S. sailors snip hair off Franklin Roosevelt's pet Scottie?

546. Who won the 1976 Republican and Democratic primaries in New Hampshire?

547. How did Thomas Jefferson break his arm and collar bone?

548. Which evangelist officiated at the burial of Lyndon Johnson?

ANSWERS

540. Andrew Jackson

541. $7 million, with operating profits of $500,000 a year

542. Ronald Reagan

543. Each eyeglass was to have two semi-circular lenses, with the lower lens having a greater magnifying strength

544. She graduated as valedictorian and May Queen

545. To keep as souvenirs of the dog's presence on a warship

546. Gerald Ford, Republican, and Jimmy Carter, Democrat

547. He fell off a galloping horse

548. Rev. Dr. Billy Graham

549. Which Presidential portrait looked down on Gerald Ford the moment he was sworn in as President?

550. What was President Truman doing when he learned that North Korea had invaded South Korea?

551. From where did the Roosevelt family originate?

552. A large map of the world hung on the wall of President Nixon's office in the Executive Office Building. Which continents, in the map, appeared in the center:
    a. Africa and Europe
    b. North and South America

553. What did Richard Nixon give Lyndon Johnson moments before the 1969 inaugural ceremony?

554. What is so uncanny about the marked floor position where John Quincy Adams had his desk in the old House of Representatives chamber in the Capitol?

ANSWERS

549. George Washington

550. Sitting in his library at Independence, Missouri, just after 10 p.m., Saturday, June 24, 1950

551. Holland

552. b) North and South America

553. A blanket, to keep warm

554. Only at this spot can one hear clearly what is merely whispered 15 yards away.

555. Who bought the Harry Truman birth place at Lamar, Missouri, and donated it to the state as an historic site?

556. Carved in the mantel of the White House State Dining Room is a quotation from a letter written by John Adams on his second night as President. In part, it reads: *"May none but honest and wise men ever rule under this roof."* Who ordered the words etched in the mantel?

557. Why was the young Abraham Lincoln so distraught that he could not bring himself to attend sessions of the Illinois State legislature?

558. Which President had a younger twin brother and sister named Randolph and Anna?

559. What great personal loss did James Monroe suffer while Governor of Virginia?

560. Name the Secret Service agent who protectively jumped on top of Lyndon Johnson after shots struck the Kennedy motorcade in Dallas.

ANSWERS

555. The United Automobile Workers.

556. Franklin Roosevelt

557. His engagement to Mary Todd had broken up, though he later married her

558. Thomas Jefferson

559. The death of his only son from "diseases of childhood"

560. Rufus Youngblood

561. Woodrow Wilson was partially blind. At what age did his left eye first become impaired?

562. Which President-elect visited 10 Central and South American countries on a good-will mission before his inauguration?

563. Which three people witnessed John Kennedy's last Will?

564. How many Articles of Impeachment had the House Judiciary Committee voted to recommend before President Nixon resigned?

565. Which Chief Executive considered Russian dictator Joseph Stalin "honest—but smart as hell"?

566. By coincidence, on the same day in 1855, two former Presidents of the U.S. sat in the gallery of the House of Commons in London, England, to listen to debates. Who were they?

567. Which President was born in a home many believe to be the oldest three-story brick house in Virginia?

ANSWERS

561. 49

562. Herbert Hoover

563. Theodore Sorensen, Evelyn Lincoln and Ted Reardon, Jr.

564. Three

565. Harry Truman, after meeting him at Potsdam, 1945

566. Martin Van Buren and Millard Fillmore

567. William Henry Harrison, born in the home built by his grandfather in 1726 at Charles City

568. Which First Family held open house on Wednesday evenings when coffee, tea and iced cakes were served?

569. What is the annual pension granted widowed spouses of former Presidents?

570. How many ballots were held before Woodrow Wilson won the Presidential nomination at the Democratic convention in Baltimore in 1912?

571. Franklin Roosevelt was editor-in-chief of which undergraduate daily paper?

572. Name the showbiz star Ronald Reagan took Nancy to see on their first date.

573. What was the name of the cocker spaniel made famous in Richard Nixon's TV speech of 1952?

574. Name the Vice President who wrote to his mother a day before he unexpectedly succeeded to the Presidency: "I'll be home one of these days......"

575. Which future President was aide-de-camp to another future President during the Civil War?

ANSWERS

568. James and Elizabeth Monroe

569. $20,000

570. 46

571. *The Harvard Crimson*

572. Sophie Tucker

573. Checkers

574. Harry Truman

575. Captain William McKinley was ADC to General Rutherford Hayes

576. When Abraham Lincoln wrote a thank you letter to General Sherman for his Christmas gift in 1864, what did he refer to?

577. Whose middle initial was nothing more than an initial?

578. What were Gerald Ford's names before his mother's remarriage and his change of names to his stepfather's?

579. Which President gave a plastic bust of himself to the Pope?

580. How tall was Theodore Roosevelt?

581. Why was Abigail Adams furious when Philadelphians invited her and the President to attend a birthday party for former President Washington?

582. What tragedies struck Thomas Jefferson in 1782 and 1784?

583. How long after Richard Nixon's letter of resignation was delivered to the Secretary of State was Gerald Ford sworn in as President?

ANSWERS

576. The capture of Savannah, Ga. by Union troops

577. Harry S Truman. It stood as a compromise for the names of his maternal and paternal grandfathers—*Solomon* Young and Anderson *Shippe* Truman

578. Leslie Lynch King

579. Lyndon Johnson

580. 5 ft. 8 in.

581. She did not think the President should play second fiddle to anyone—including George Washington

582. His wife, Martha, died in 1782 and two years later their daughter, Lucy, died of whooping cough

583. 28 minutes

584. What percentage of the popular vote was won by independent Ross Perot in the 1992 election?

585 Who was the first daughter of an incumbent President to have her wedding outside the White House?

586. What is the annual salary, exclusive of expenses and other allowances, granted the President?

587. What was the nationality of the nurse who cared for President Kennedy's children?

588. Which surgeon conducted the postmortem on Abraham Lincoln and then, 16 years later, attended President Garfield as he lay dying from an assassin's bullet?

589. Who was Harry Truman's running mate in 1948?

590. How did Abraham Lincoln's son, Robert, show his appreciation to a Congressman for pressing so hard for funds to build the Lincoln Memorial?

ANSWERS

584. 19%, though he did not carry a single state

585. Luci Baines Johnson, whose wedding was held at the Shrine of the Immaculate Conception, Washington, D.C. 1966

586. Doubled to $400,000 as of January 2001

587. English

588. J.J. Woodward

589. Alben W. Barkley

590. He gave him the original manuscript of Abraham Lincoln's speech delivered outside the White House after the 1864 election

591. In which city was Theodore Roosevelt sworn in as 26th President?

592. Which of his relatives did President Kennedy appoint to head The Peace Corps?

593. This college student filed the names of new acquaintances on index cards.

594. What was the name given to President Reagan's ranch near Santa Barbara, California?

595. Where did President Ford pray shortly before pardoning Richard Nixon?

596. What is so historic about a rifle with the serial number C2766?

597. Which First Lady strived unsuccessfully to have her husband appoint the first woman to the Supreme Court?

598. Whom did Harry Truman want to be the Democratic Party's nominee for President in 1956?

ANSWERS

591. Buffalo, N.Y.

592. His brother-in-law, Sargent Shriver, husband of Eunice Kennedy

593. Bill Clinton did this while studying at Oxford University on a prestigious Rhodes Scholarship

594. Rancho del Cielo

595. St. John's Church, opposite the White House

596. It was the Manlicher-Carcano Italian military rifle fired by Lee Harvey Oswald to assassinate President Kennedy

597. Lady Bird Johnson

598. Averell Harriman

599. What was the code name for the D-Day landings commanded by Dwight Eisenhower?

600. Where did President Kennedy dine off gold-rimmed china given by the City of Paris to Napoleon as a coronation gift?

601. Whom did Richard Nixon defeat in his U.S. Senate race in 1950?

602. How did Jimmy Carter's son, James Earl Carter, get nicknamed *Chip*?

603. What color were Dwight Eisenhower's eyes?

604. What song did the bands play when Harry Truman returned to Washington, D.C. the victor in the 1948 election?

605. What code name did the Secret Service give Vice President Rockefeller?

606. Which Chief Executive wrote that "power in Washington is measured by how much access a person has to the President"?

ANSWERS

599. Operation *Overlord*

600. At the Palace of Versailles, France

601. Helen Gahagan Douglas

602. Nurses at the hospital in Oahu, Hawaii, gave it to him when he was born there

603. Blue

604. *I'm Just Wild About Harry*

605. Sand Storm

606. Gerald Ford

607. The State Department has a state drawing room proclaimed by connoisseurs as "the most beautiful 18th century style American drawing room in the United States." After which President is it named?

608. What ominous news did Richard Nixon read on Fathers' Day 1972?

609. When did Franklin Roosevelt make his last Will?

610. On the eve of what historic day did President Truman take up residence for the first time in the White House?

611. Where did Woodrow Wilson die?

612. How often during the Eisenhower administration did Vice President Nixon preside over meetings of the Cabinet and the National Security Council?

613. Which President was present at the dedication of the most popular museum in the country, the Smithsonian's Air & Space Museum?

ANSWERS

607. John Quincy Adams

608. A newspaper report stating that five men had been arrested in the Democratic National Committee headquarters at the Watergate

609. Two weeks before the Japanese attack on Pearl Harbor

610. May 7, 1945, the day before V-E Day

611. In his home at 2340 S St., N.W., Washington, D.C.

612. 19 Cabinet meetings and 26 NSC meetings

613. Gerald Ford

614. What job did Dwight Eisenhower have when he moved to 60 Morningside Drive, Morningside Heights, New York City?

615. What is the radio call sign for the Presidential helicopter?

616. Guess who described the White House as "a nice prison, but a prison nevertheless."

617. On which Washington, D.C. monument are the following words inscribed: "I have sworn upon the altar of God, eternal hostility against every form of tyranny over the mind of men"?

618. How many copies sold in the first week of the book, *Redneck Power: The Wit and Wisdom of Billy Carter*?

619. Where was Eleanor Roosevelt when she took a phone call to return to the White House, where she learned of her husband's death?

620. What was the population of the U.S. at the time Thomas Jefferson became President?

ANSWERS

614. President of Columbia University

615. Marine One

616. Harry Truman

617. The Jefferson Memorial

618. 210,000

619. At the Sulgrave Club, Washington, D.C.

620. 5.3 million

621. Name the President who was so bored while posing for a portrait that the painter was appalled by the look on his face.

622. What gambling game did Richard Nixon learn en route to the South Pacific in 1943?

623. Which spouse of which former President had a premonition of his death a week before he died?

624. Long before he became President this man hitchhiked to a teacher's college to get a part-time job and to study. Who was he?

625. Which weak and asthmatic child grew into a sturdy and vigorous President?

626. Who signed a petition while a student at the College of William and Mary, Williamsburg, Va., complaining of "scarce and intolerable food"?

627. Name the sister of a future President who married into one of England's leading aristocratic families.

ANSWERS

621. Gilbert Stuart was appalled by George Washington's gaze

622. Poker

623. Julia Tyler dreamed of danger to her husband, John's life

624. Lyndon Johnson

625. Theodore Roosevelt

626. James Monroe

627. Kathleen Kennedy, sister of John, married the Marquis of Hartington, heir to the Duke of Devonshire

QUESTIONS

628. Why did the Governor General of Australia tip Herbert Hoover five shillings?

629. The 2000 Presidential election gave George W. Bush 50,456,002 votes (47.87%) and Al Gore 50,999,897 votes (48.38%). What were the electoral college votes won by each?

630. When did John F. Kennedy begin to suffer from life-long back pain?

631. How did 3-year-old Calvin Coolidge break his arm?

632. What did the WIN campaign buttons stand for when launched in the first days of Gerald Ford's presidency?

633. Who was Chancellor of the University of Buffalo from its founding until his death?

634. Who starred with Ronald Reagan in the 1938 movie, *Brother Rat?*

635. Which President became father-in-law to his own private secretary?

ANSWERS

628. Hoover, then a mining engineer in Australia, had just escorted the visitor down a shaft

629. Bush 271, Gore 266

630. During a football scrimmage at Harvard

631. He fell off a horse

632. Whip Inflation Now

633. Millard Fillmore

634. His first wife, Jane Wyman

635. James Monroe, after his wife's nephew, Samuel Gouverneur, married the President's younger daughter, Maria Hester

636. Which future President won the orator's prize at the University of Virginia when arguing against the question: "Is the Roman Catholic Church a menace to American institutions?"?

637. Aboard which warships did Franklin Roosevelt and Winston Churchill sail off the coast of Newfoundland before issuing the *Atlantic Charter* of common beliefs?

638. To which Washington, D.C. school did Richard Nixon send his daughters?

639. What movie, shown at the White House in 1945, brought tears to the eyes of Harry Truman?

640. Which future President fulfilled a promise to work two weeks on a dairy farm if he won election to Congress at his first try?

641. How old was Lyndon Johnson when the White House approved his appointment as regional head of the National Youth Administration in Texas?

642. Whose father had his house seized after the 1929 stock market crash because he could not meet the mortgage payments?

ANSWERS

636. Woodrow Wilson

637. The American cruiser *Augusta* and the British battleship *Prince of Wales*

638. Sidwell Friends School

639. *Springtime*, starring Jeannette MacDonald

640. Gerald Ford

641. 27

642. Gerald Ford

643. Who gave the bride away at Franklin Roosevelt's wedding?

644. Who was the first person to tell Rose Kennedy that her son, the President, had been shot?

645. When was the Jefferson Memorial dedicated in Washington, D.C.?

646. Which famous detective was a son-in-law of President Chester Arthur?

647. Which future President turned down the post of New York City's Commissioner of Street Cleaning?

648. Which future President was so homesick as a pre-teen student that he walked the 14 miles home?

649. Why did President James Polk refuse to accept the credentials of the Austrian Ambassador?

650. What happened to the child, Jimmy Carter, after he shot his sister in the rear with a BB gun?

ANSWERS

643. Incumbent President Theodore Roosevelt, her uncle

644. The family chauffeur, Frank Saunders

645. 1943

646. Allan Pinkerton

647. Theodore Roosevelt

648. Franklin Pierce

649. Because the diplomat called at the White House on a Sunday

650. His father whipped him

651. Name the Presidential Press Secretary who died at his desk as he prepared to answer reporters' questions.

652. How many countries had Richard Nixon visited by the time he ran for President in 1960?

653. How did Harry Truman's childhood cat get his name, *Bob*?

654. For how many minutes did John Kennedy speak during his inaugural address?

655. He tossed horseshoes to relax.

656. Which of his successors did President Andrew Johnson put down with the comment that "his brain could have been compressed within the periphery of a nutshell"?

657. Who had given Jimmy Carter the Bible which he chose to use during his swearing-in ceremony?

658. What percentage of the popular votes cast did Richard Nixon win in his landslide victory over George McGovern in 1972?

ANSWERS

651. Charles Ross, press secretary to Truman

652. 54

653. A piece of coal singed off his tail

654. 14

655. George H.W. Bush

656. President Ulysses S. Grant

657. His mother

658. 60.7 per cent